AGGRESSIVE
MERCY

Kilian McDonnell, OSB

SAINT JOHN'S UNIVERSITY PRESS

COLLEGEVILLE, MINNESOTA

Cover design by Alan Reed, OSB.

Library of Congress Cataloging-in-Publication Data

McDonnell, Kilian.
    [Poems. Selections]
    Aggressive Mercy / Kilian McDonnell.
      pages   cm
    ISBN 978-0-9884075-5-8 (paperback)
    1. Christian poetry, American.   I. Title.
PS3613.C3878A6   2014
811'.6—dc23   2014000275

"Father Kilian McDonnell's new book of collected poems has the right title—*Aggressive Mercy*. The seventy-three poems give consistent evidence of the poet's focus and conviction of the realities of an unnamable, incomprehensible Mercy, a 'given' that is 'extravagant beyond beyondness,' that one questions but relies on, and that permeates the biblical phrases through which he speaks. Fr. Kilian speaks as Mary, or Jacob, or Lazarus or Judas's wife. He speaks from their torment and their ordinariness. From their bewilderment. At the Annunciation, Mary is wiping up a mess on the kitchen floor with a rag when light breaks into her life. It is encountering a different Annunciation from what we are used to: it could be us, stunned by the 'glory of the preposterous.'

"There is no room for a doubt in these poems that we humans are inclined to 'minor treacheries' and 'small mess[es].' We make 'unbalanced vows' which mysteriously bind the Lord 'while we are free / to plunge a dagger / into the heart of Love.' Moses, for example, moves toward the 'summit,' where 'Unseeing / in the presence of the Invisible / unknowing while beholding the Unknowable' he waits. We do not have minds that can 'lay hold God's whole,' and this God cannot be 'packaged.' We have only 'the backlit blood of Yahweh's / fingers.' We are 'the yawning sated' keen for 'the great gulps of the world.' Father Kilian struggles with our 'Numb fidelity' and our 'extinguished fire,' but he reassures himself, and us, that 'Cold desire is still desire.' Throughout these searching poems, Father Kilian wonders about 'the difference / between living / in God's glory / and walking / in God's shadow.'"

Kathryn Hohlwein
President and Founder of The Readers of Homer

"In his inimitable style, Kilian brings biblical characters and his fellow monks to life in poetic vignettes without airbrushing their flawed humanity. In this, he has no peer. Not even God always escapes the candor Kilian brings to his perceptions. With a mere phrase or short sentence he gives readers an amazing sensory feel for the realism of personages and their environments.

"By his own admission, Kilian does not write 'pious poems,' thus leaving readers totally free to experience the less than genteel, fully human reactions among his characters. One can imagine the twinkle in his eyes as he composes many of these poems. But caution is in order: with superb irony, Kilian often ends the episodes with sneaky little 'depth charges' exploding beneath the surface of entertainment, astonishing and provoking his readers in unanticipated ways."

A. Regina Schulte

"Kilian McDonnell's *Aggressive Mercy* charms the reader with the voice of a seasoned poet at the top of his game and a monk in late life who still has a few arguments to settle with God and cannot resist the temptation to rewrite a few lines of Scripture. McDonnell retells the old stories from Genesis to Acts in clear, colloquial language that gives back to his characters from Adam to Mary and the Apostles a credible humanity and along the way offers the reader autobiographical vignettes from his own life. These are poems of faith that belong in the library of the heart."

Nick Hayes
Professor of History and University Chair
  in Critical Thinking
St. John's University
Collegeville, Minnesota
Author of *One Fine Morning:*
  Memories of My Father

"*Aggressive Mercy* is an unapologetic inquisition of Scripture, God, and humanity. Kilian McDonnell pits his unparalleled knowledge of our biblical heritage against the tough questions and painful truths necessary for a life of faith. God is not perfect, but is humanized and fallible. Even Jesus holds God accountable, teaching us that we, too, might question our creator: 'You called me, / walked away / ignored my pleas / and left me alone / nails in my hands. / You left me alone.' McDonnell teaches us that questions and doubts are, in fact, the birthplace of faith: 'But you know our hearts from afar, you know we stutter and we stumble.' Beautifully lyric, unwaveringly honest, and immeasurably brave, this collection gives us the gift of a new way to read our history and ourselves."

Sivan Butler-Rotholz
Editor, *As It Ought to Be;*
Founder, *Reviving Herstory*

To the memory of my mother and father,
Dorothea (Dora) Auerbach
and Joseph P. McDonnell,
who raised eight children and, as far as I know,
never quarreled

CONTENTS

PART III

PART IV

PART I

THE HAWK SWOOPS

Where can I go from your spirit? Psalm 139:7

You count our wanderings West;
tell our staggerings East.
Like a hawk, you eye us

from afar. When you swoop low,
your shadow covers us
before we hear your wings go *swish*.

If we crawl into the rocks,
you eye us from the top of the pine
and wait for us

to show our heads
to forage for food.
When we hide under cover

of the weeping willows
at the waterfall,
you're not deceived

as we've hidden there before.
If we explore Maine's forests,
you fly so high,

you eye us through
the canopy. As for me,
when I see you

through the lattice
scratching on my door
with your talons
my failings so terrify me
I hide in the cellar, imagine
you'll lift latch and kill.

Wrong.
Your mercy stalks me.

GOD HOLDING OUT
A BEGGAR'S HAND

O the depth of the riches and wisdom and knowledge
of God! Romans 11:33

Should a princess trust a prince
who vows his deathless love knows
no bounds and swears the flawless,
off-white pearls he strings

around her neck
are the very same King Solomon gave
the Queen of Sheba in 930 BC?
Who would believe

we send away with shrugs
the one who lies in wait
behind our tattered smelly lives
with loot for us

from a thousand heavens?
Eye has not seen,
ear has not heard,
nor the heart imagined,

extravagance beyond beyondness,
that cache in the well of God's heart
no plumb line can touch.
Who would believe God

gives away gold bullion
with professional absurdity
but extends a vagrant's hand
begging for our love?

ODE TO ADAM AND EVE
AND DESCENDANTS

I praise you, for I am fearfully and wonderfully made.
Psalm 139:14

Gathered from the dust,
a little spittle
added for binding
to keep the trouble together.

Given to itches,
pains in the head,
fallen arches
and flatulence.

Still, scrape away the crud,
well proportioned,
the angles are right,
a certain symmetry:

two eyes on different sides
of one nose, the mouth
mostly horizontal,
a not too accommodating chin.

Back before clocks
began to measure movement,
Yahweh spared a single breath
from vast eternal lungs

and breathed it hot,
like molten gold,
to give it starch,

imparted a spasm
of God's own life,
the disquiet of longing,
a reach to touch beyond,

gave it shards
of non-specific anguish,
like a stormy dawn
struggling toward the day.

In fact, in spite of a crooked nose,
made a little less than angels,
an image, now lightly skewed,
of the one who bent

to breathe upon the worry.
I sing a new song to the muck
and wonder of our being.

ABRAM HAS WOMEN TROUBLE

Then Sarai said to Abram, May the wrong done to me
be on you! *Genesis 16:5*

I was minding my own business,
patting my camel's neck
as it farted contentedly
and drank from the murky Balikh
when I heard God say, *Go,*
unmistakable
as an arrow in the gut.
I'm to leave the graves
of my ancestors to go
to a land he does not trouble himself
to name. God promises
my seventy-five-year-old seed
will sprout a sturdy son
in Sarai's sixty-five-year-old
womb, barren as the Dead Sea.

Sarai pulls up the tent pegs,
harnesses our camel
and with our other beasts
we set off in the direction
of nowhere.

For decades the Lord yawns,
picks at the old scab
on his elbow, dithers with his hoe
in the cactus garden rather
than deliver on his promise
of a son.

Thinking I'm asleep
Sarai weeps her gall into our pillow
and in the morning suggests
God is not reliable
and we should act,
not wait for God.

I should sleep with Hagar,
her Egyptian slave.

And the child would belong
to Sarai.

That evening
Sarai unrolls my sleeping carpet,
lays the eager Hagar
where she herself had slept
and calls me in.

When Hagar blossoms
she flaunts her protruding belly
to the four corners of the tent,
wherever Sarai shows
her face.

Tears and recriminations.

So now it is my fault.

THE CHOSEN

When her [Rachel's] time to give birth was at hand, there were twins in her womb. The first came out red, all his body like a hairy mantle; so they named him Esau. Afterward his brother came out, with his hand gripping Esau's heel; so he was named Jacob. Genesis 25:24-26

Why would the Lord come
to me in a dream, lean a ladder
against the edge of heaven

with angels climbing up and down
and the terrible I AM standing
at my side? Neither godly man

nor reliable, I, Jacob, mother's pet,
girl-like forearms, to my shame,
plan to glue lamb wool on my arms

so I will feel like hairy Esau
to my blind and gasping Father.
I lie to him as death rattles

in his throat.
                    I always thought God
irrelevant but now he pushes his way in.
This uninvited guest makes promises

to be with me no matter where I go,
will multiply my seed, bring me back
to this trembling sacred spot

which is rancid with old incense
and God. But He leaves me faded holiness
chewing lemon rinds. I'm afraid.

If God will be with me, if
he will give me bread to eat, if
he will give me clothing to wear,
then the Lord shall be my God.

LEAD US NOT INTO TEMPTATION

. . . the elder shall serve the younger. Genesis 25:23

The God of tenderness lays a long sword
between twin Esau and me while we wrestle
around umbilical cords in mother's

amniotic seas, we wrestle to see who will exit first.
The wise Lord falters when he decrees Esau
shall birth first but the older shall serve

the younger. This canker creates our dysfunctional
brotherhood. I, the less equal twin,
do what I can and grab Esau by the heel

so when the midwife pulls him out
she pulls me too. But always this aching
anger in my heart.
                    Esau becomes a hunter

and bandit. He smells of the forest,
whose one thrust spear
will fell the ibex, while I'm the herder,

the quiet one, at home I love to sit
on camel-hair cushions and compose harp music
for my mother. Like a king I'm ripe with aroma

of fresh myrrh and new smoke from frankincense.
—Decrees have consequences
as surely as fish stinks after three days

in the bottom of the boat. If father Isaac
loves his ape-armed Esau
more than me, Jacob, of baby-bottom skin,

if Father gives Esau his prize sheep
and me his stinking goats, if Mother
and I must kneel in puddles when Esau passes,
has God not led us into temptation?

MINIMAL EXPECTATIONS

*I am no longer worthy to be called your son; treat me like one
of your hired hands.* Luke 15:19

I, Jacob, twenty-one, muscle man,
hot shot, not a drachma to my name,
feed the gentile's hogs the swill I crave:
dead flies, dead beetles float upon the scum.

A year ago I had asked my father, hale
at fifty-five, for my portion now. He gave it.
At dawn I left for brighter lights, louder songs,
faster ladies. But lights grow dim,

songs fade, at sunup the ladies want
their drachmas and a tip. Depravity's dear.
I cannot still the noises of my heart:
Go home, you selfish bastard, face your shame.

*Petition father for a servant's wage;
you're no longer fit to be a son.* As I walk,
how can I name my shame?
I need to find the right words.

Far-off I see a man whose gait I recognize,
who's out of breath because he runs
to take me in his arms: his tears drown
the naming of my sin. Father stammers his love

and shouts, *Call in the gang, we're going*
to celebrate with flow of wine
till the sheepskin's dead. The stars will dance
cheek to cheek until the dew is fresh upon the grass

and the sun sneezes. He removes the ring
his father gave him, slips it on my finger;
calls for lambskin sandals, a robe of silk
with silver shoulder clasp inset with green jade.

THE ARK OF THE COVENANT

The anger of the LORD was kindled against Uzzah; and God struck him there because he reached out his hand to the ark [to steady it]; and he died there beside the ark of God. David was angry because the LORD had burst forth with an outburst upon Uzzah. 2 Samuel 6:7-8

A box, a gold mercy seat
on top, and two facing
cherubim whose wings
overshadow the throne.

Two poles overlain
with gold through two
rings overlain with gold,
for carrying. From here

God moves with and speaks
to Israel. Still a spiky sort,
like cuddling an anointed
porcupine.

Will not be packaged.
Very difficult.
Laid back, yes,
but not compliant.

Travels at your will,
but not on your terms.
Will not be casually touched,
strikes the careless hand

which tries to steady it,
knows worth divine.
Accepts prostrations,
bending of the knee,

road side sacrifices,
incense. When captive,
a hostile trophy, bestows
bubonic plagues,

dysentery, boils,
hemorrhoids. When used
as magic, gives glorious
undoing, battles lost,
thirty thousand fall.
As I said, very difficult,
sensitive, cannot
be managed, but God moves

with the Ark when Israel moves,
icon of power, where Yahweh
speaks of stable mercy and images
the glory of the preposterous.

RETIREMENT HOME CHAPEL

In old age [the righteous] still produce fruit; they are always green and full of sap. Psalm 92:14

God lives down the corridor,
last door on the left. At five
we bring the wine pressed

from stumbling years
of blazing mediocrity
and small victories.

For bread, the mud cakes
of our days, carefully baked
in minor treacheries.

These gifts we lay upon the altar
and see God bending over
our small mess with infinite delight.

UNEQUAL EQUALS

[God] said to him [Abram], Bring me a heifer three
years old. *Genesis 15:9*

God tells me to cut
a three-year heifer
in two, laying each half

over against the other.
He extends a bony hand
and grasps mine. We walk

hand in hand between
the bleeding halves
in pledge of mutual fidelity.

If I am unfaithful,
God can cut me in two.
But God presses not his claim.

I can always come back.
If God is unfaithful,
I can cut God in two.

COVENANT COMPULSION
OF THE PIT-BULL

*God made covenants with Noah, David, the Israelites
in general, and renewed covenants several times with
Abraham, Josiah, and Nehemiah.*

God insecure?
Why does God initiate
these constant bondings

in blood and fire
with a solemn oath
of fidelity, unbalanced vows

which bind the Lord
while we are free
to plunge a dagger

into the heart of Love
without
ripping up the pact?

We always can come back
on our knees to find
God has opened the door.

He takes the first step.
This pit-bull-God sinks teeth
into our leg, no clubbing

with Leviathan's jaw bone
ever unclenches.
Was love ever so desperate?

WHERE LIGHT—THERE DEEPEST DARK

You shall see my back; but my face shall not be seen. Exodus 33:23

By taking flesh God makes himself understood only by appearing still more incomprehensible.

Maximus the Confessor, *Ambigua*

Baby we understand. Young mother,
swaddling clothes, and manger
are simple truths, not beyond us.
But original life unpackaged, the imageless

made Image, laid where cows feed?
The improbable tango of fire and straw,
the unthinkable coupling of lightning
and flesh? Where Light leaps down

to flesh—is touchable—there the deepest
Nubian black, the glittering dark,
like Yahweh setting Moses in rock's cleft,
and putting his palm over him, lest he see

from the front his naked glory and die.
Through the backlit blood of Yahweh's
fingers, Moses sees shadows moving.
Then Yahweh takes his hand away

as he marches by and Moses sees his back
walking North, like the black I saw
when, young fool, I looked straight
into Sturgeon Point's lighthouse beam.

DOWN IN THE ORDINARY

What now is the meaning of Moses' entry into the darkness and the vision of God that he enjoyed? . . . The true vision and the true knowledge of what we seek consists precisely in not seeing, in an awareness that our goal transcends all knowledge and is everywhere cut off from us by the darkness of incomprehensibility. Gregory of Nyssa, The Life of Moses

Out of a cloud God calls Moses
to ascend Mount Sinai.
He stumbles up the slope to the pinnacle.
He feels the air thin and he pants.

Toward the top he draws near
the darkness covering the summit
where God dwells. Trembling,
Moses steps into the holiness and terror,

eyes blinded by excess of glory,
as if archangels had exploded
ten thousand suns. Unseeing
in the presence of the Invisible,

unknowing while beholding the Unknowable,
he remains forty days and forty nights
in spite of the danger
of his groping violating the Presence.

Then Moses lurches down the mountain
into the ordinary carrying the glow
of God's glory on his face, the drops
of night in his eyes, and in his arms

two stone tablets on which
God's right finger wrote
ten covenant commandments.
When the glow fades, he recollects

that while standing at the top
in the dazzling dark, his mind could not
lay hold God's whole, but now in the ordinary
he grasps for the first time,
he can never stand outside of God.

THE DARK NIGHT OF THE HEART

He made darkness his covering around him, his canopy thick clouds dark with water. Psalm 18:11

Like all seducers, you despise
the one you led to bed.

You pull down the tent
upon me, and walk away.

All I wanted was to sit beside you,
dip my bread into your cup.

Now it is always three o'clock
in the morning and no moon shines.

Did you test me when the dark cloud
overshadowed me, to see if I'd serve you

for nothing? Lord, you spoke soft words
of comfort, led me to the bed,

seduced me in the evening,
forsook me in the morning.

URIAH, HITTITE, MAN OF HONOR

So David sent messengers to get her [Bathsheba], and she came
to him, and he lay with her. . . . The woman conceived; and she
sent and told David, I am pregnant. *2 Samuel 11:4, 5*

Commander Joab sends me to Jerusalem
to report to King David on the war
against the Ammonites. Strange: Joab picks me,
one of the king's Mighty Men, a general,

to carry news. Why a general for a soldier's task,
like using a battering ram to topple a tent?
King David receives me as a long-lost brother,
offers flagons of wine while we discuss

the strategies of war as though I were
Joab. After five flagons the King says
Go home to wash your feet (go home
and bed your wife), sends meat and wine

and almond cakes from the King's table
for a grand feast with Bathsheba. But the code
of honor asks why a soldier should enjoy the rapture
of deep flesh while comrades pour out

their guts in war. Kings forget, so I bed
at the king's gate with other servants. Next day
King David asks where I slept, seems surprised
I slept at the gate but invites me to sup with him.

He toasts his dead horse, his faithful dog, my horse,
the Sea of Galilee, Mount Sinai and the fig tree
in his garden. Cross-eyed, I stumble
to the King's gate to sleep. Next morning

the King asks again where I slept. He sends me
back to fight Ammonites with a letter in my hand
for Commander Joab. Probably suggests
Joab use the military strategies we discussed
while sipping his best wine.

DAVID AND ABSALOM

Now in all Israel there was no one to be praised so much for his beauty as Absalom; from the sole of his foot to the crown of his head there was no blemish in him. . . . Absalom got himself a chariot and horses, and fifty men to run ahead of him. . . . The conspiracy grew in strength, and the people with Absalom kept increasing. 2 Samuel 14:25; 15:1, 12

In David's bed at Hebron troubles sleep
between the sheets: can six fair sons of six
fair wives run free while only one will keep
the crown, the others sip their wine as the torch
burns low? Now Absalom, third-born son
of David, out of Maacah from Geshur,
is fairer than his other sons, and none
in Israel stands comelier. No blur,
no blemish in the mirror when he combs
his hair. No soldier kept his mane as long,
or at year's end, when cut, would weigh the tresses
like blessed relics to which reverences belong.
But Absalom keeps his limit as he keeps
his hair: waits, watches, while another sleeps.

When Amnon, first among the princes, raped
his sister Tamar, then despised her, the king
was royally angry, but the heir escaped
his wrath. Amnon drank wine in peace. Could
   David bring
the prince's shame to light? And brother dear,
the comely Absalom, kept silent, gave

no hints of vengeance. But those who hold the
    spear
to guard the gate, and the Hittite cousins of dead
Uriah knew that errant regal sex
will sluice to death like summer torrents down
the Wadi Musa. Brother Absalom collects
Tamar's tears like brilliant rubies for a crown.
She rips her gown, puts ashes on her head,
laments the lasting stain of brother's bed.

By slow and silent turns through two long years
Absalom plans his strike. He's hunter with a snare.
He invites the princes of the realm, when fears
are numb, to celebrate with him and share
the dancing when the shearing of the sheep
at Baal-hazor is finished. When every heart
is bleary in the tangled wildness of the deep
red wine, the host then rises as to start
a toast, with goblets full and lifted high,
the sober Absalom with one quick thrust
dispatches Amnon to Sheol—To die
for family lust is doubly shame. But just—
Each tipsy prince locates his mule and rides
from where the tribal blood will wave like tides.

For three long years the son escaped the rage
of David's wrath in mother's feathered nest
in far Geshur, until of very age
the anger slowly dies in David's breast.

Besides, the king now yearns for Absalom.
The bloodied son returned to David's court,
in quiet dropping here a crumb, there a plum,
and planning treacheries by making sport
of justice at the city gate. Ere
plaintiffs come to David he gives
gentle judgments, soft replies, swears
attention to their needs, their guilt forgives
with kisses on the claimant's hand:
"If only I were judge—you understand."

He rises early, gets himself some steeds
and chariots and fifty men to run
before him, winning hearts and sewing seeds
of revolution, seeds that need no sun,
but grow as well when dark. For four long years
he plants his discontent. And only then
Absalom tells the king he wishes to appear
before the Lord in Hebron where pious men
fulfill their vows (and where the soldiers first
proclaimed his father King of Judah). While
between his bows and ablutions, his hair
already gathered close as is the style,
the prince sends secret word "Rise up, and sound
the cry: 'In Hebron Absalom is crowned.'"

The hearts and chariots of Israel
run after Absalom, two hundred men
from David's city. Faulty noses can smell

rebellion. David gives the sign of when
to flee Jerusalem and leaves with all
his house except for two of David's priests,
and ten less favored concubines—a small
contingent keeping palace walls—not least,
not last, the Ark. The king goes weeping down
the Kedron Valley, barefoot up the Mount
of Olives. David has scarcely left the town
when Absalom rides in and can dismount
as Israel's king. For all the land now rushes
to bow and bend the knee. No one blushes.

To make it clear, no turning back, that rule
has passed to Absalom, fixed and firm,
the newest king gives orders no fool
could possibly mistake. By sperm
he will confirm his claim. For all to see,
a tent is pitched upon the palace roof
from which his Dad had seen Bathsheba. (She
was Eve in Eden.) Absalom gives proof
of kingship, nailing risky memories
by bedding father's concubines, from one
to ten, in such a place, with such an ease.
The rupture is complete; the battle won.
This story of the tent is swagger told
as the son is recognized as father's cuckold.

But in the dark devouring forest war
near Ephraim, David's army wins, and he

tells Joab: "Please, I beg, do not ignore
a father's feelings; for sake of me,
deal gently with the boy." Now riding fast
along the forest paths the flowing hair
of Absalom is snagged as he rides past
a lower branch that leaves him hanging there
like a hog strung up for slaughter, the mule
proceeding through the thickets all alone.
But Joab snubs both David and his rule
(Beware the blanket lying near the throne),
takes three long spears to pierce the rebel breast.
Death by hair. Rebellion brought to rest.

The men are bearing Absalom on high,
His hair hangs down, the badge of his excess.
They throw his body in a pit nearby,
and pile a heap of stones. Of this success
what fool will risk the wrath to tell the king?
A Cushite foreigner blurts out the news.
All fades to nullity. Everything.
The father/king forgets: the public use
of concubines, from one to ten, forgets
revolt and shame, forgets all those who died
for him, the war he won, forgets the threats.
"No . . . I would have died for you, my son.

Died for you, O no, O Absalom."

PART II

THE FAMILY TREE OF JESUS

Judah the father of Perez and Zerah by Tamar. Matthew 1:3

Truth, like life, is in the blood
where lies cannot hide.
No sly erasures, no dodges.

Matthew keeps his tax rolls
clean, knows who's paid,
who still owes, what goes

to Caesar, what to God.
Knows not to falsify the books.
When he lists thirty-nine

begots of Jesus' ancestors,
he keeps the shame that herders
recite at night around the Galilean fires.

Twice-spurned Tamar,
disguised as Judah's whore during
sheep shearing beside the road

to Bethlehem. She asks a signet,
cord and staff as pledge
on future payment. Slut Rahab

built her house into the city wall
for ease of egress, uses a crimson cord
in the window as earnest of future payment

by Joshua's men sent to spy the land.
As earnest Uriah's wife Bathsheba bathed
upon the roof, David saw, lusted,

quickly bedded, quicker dispatched husband,
to war front carrying his death
in David's letter hidden in his helmet.

Solomon, triumphant in his riddles,
glorious in his temple, wise in his palaces,
dumb in seven hundred wives,

three hundred concubines.
Behold the roots of the Jesus tree
where tainted blood speaks to purest blood.
The purging flows within.

IN THE KITCHEN

In the sixth month the angel Gabriel . . . Luke 1:26

Giotto has it wrong.
I was not kneeling
on my satin cushion
quietly at prayer,

head slightly bent.
Painters always
skew the scene,
as though my life
were wrapped in silks,

in temple smells.
Actually I had just
come back from the well.
Placing the pitcher on the table
I bumped against the edge,

spilling water on the floor.
As I bent to wipe
it with a rag,
there was a light
against the kitchen wall

as though someone had opened
the door to the sun.
Rag in hand,
hair across my face,
I turned to see

who was entering,
unannounced, uninvited.
All I saw
was light, white
against the timbers.

I heard a voice.
Greetings were given:
the Lord was with me,
I was elected,
I will conceive the Son

of God by the Holy Spirit.
My son will reign forever.

I stood afraid.

Someone closed the door.

I dropped the rag.

EVERY CHOICE
SIGNS AWAY TOMORROW

In the sixth month the angel Gabriel was sent by God to a
town in Galilee called Nazareth. Luke 1:26

Pregnant
before the bridal bed.

As village women pass
sudden silences.

At the well girls my age stand back
as I pull the leather bucket from below.

At market when I reach
across the onions

for fresh pomegranates,
whispers, sideways glances,

The girls: aghast and thrilled.
—How long has this been going on?—

In synagogue, no one sits beside me.
Joseph, appointed lector, reads the text

of Leviticus: *They shall not marry a whore,*
or a woman who has been defiled.

Archangel Gabriel silent,
God absent.

THE WHORING DAUGHTER

*When his [Jesus'] mother Mary had been engaged to
Joseph, but before they lived together, she was found
to be with child from the Holy Spirit. Matthew 1:18*

You see, Mother,
while I was busy
in the kitchen
with a pitcher

of water I'd brought
from the well, an angel

of light appeared
to say the Holy Spirit

would overshadow and rest
upon me to make a child

within my womb without
the seed of any man. The boy

will be the Son of God
and his reign will never end.

That's why my belly bulges.
Mother, please, it's true.

INFIDELITY

*Her husband Joseph, being a righteous man and unwilling to
expose her to public disgrace, planned to dismiss her quietly.*
Matthew 1:19

You can't be serious, Mary.
Me believe this staggering impossibility?!

I'm not a fool. An angel and the Holy Spirit!
Like saying the full moon planted seed
in your womb while you were trimming lamps.
You tremble knowing I don't believe it.

Well . . . you can be sure I'll not expose you.
But you must see I cannot bring you
into my home. I weep to say it,
but I'll not be coming by.

A CHRISTMAS LULLABY

Then Joseph got up, took the child and his mother by night, and went to Egypt, and remained there until the death of Herod. Matthew 2:14-15

At midnight a Sunni father
and a Shiite mother

cradling a newborn
slip out doors, sneak down

the narrow street, away
from soldiers, severed arms

and legs, creep past bomb craters,
hospital ruins, dead babies,

fugitives searching for their Egypt.
Tanks rumble through Bethlehem.

RESPONSIBILITY?

Child, why have you treated us like this? Luke 2:48

Irresponsible! Why didn't we check?
And now twenty stadia down the road
we discover he's not among our relatives.

We've been up and down the lines
three times. Guilt and panic eat like acid.
Dumb hens do not lose their chicks.

Dazed, we stumble back to Jerusalem
and for three days panic from bazaar
to the Tower of David, to the camel pens,

to Mount of Olives, to Damascus Gate—
nothing. Desperate, we enter the temple.
And there in the portico of the outer court

a twelve-year-old scholar sits at ease
among the learned of Israel. Stupefied,
we stand beside a column partially hidden

as he asks questions about Israel's worship
of stone gods on high places, complains
of fresh offal on the temple floor, refutes

the high priest on origins of wave offerings.
Whence this Torah depth? At home, an ordinary
    boy.
Finally, he sees us and comes over. *Son,*

how could you be so irresponsible?
We've searched Jerusalem for three days.
Without hesitation, *Didn't you know*

I'd be busy in my Father's house
with tasks beyond my family,
our kitchen table and the Nazareth road?
But let's go home.

SHANGHAI-ED BY A PRIEST

Whoever does not take up the cross and follow me is not worthy of me. Matthew 10:38

For Lent give up something, or take on
something to share in Jesus' bleeding.
I'll not give up seeing movies

at the Rialto. But I could skimp on sleep.
Rise 6:15, serve Mass 7:00 in the basement
of Pastor Jerry O'Donahue's rectory.

Chasuble dirty, stole tattered.
Punctual Mrs. Kaufman kneeling
on the cold concrete beside

me rattling her pink rosary.
7:30 I receive the body of Christ.
8:00, high school geometry, etc.

After Easter the same. O'Donahue
suspicious I want to be a priest. Not a word
to me but Pastor talks to Mom and Dad.

"He's said nothing to us, but we'll talk
with him." After band practice
they're waiting for me on the sofa as though

I'd flunked my algebra. "Can't a guy go
to Mass without you shipping him
off to a seminary?"

BELIEVERS AND DOUBTERS

*. . . the unclean spirit . . . ran and bowed down before
him [Jesus]; and he [unclean spirit] shouted at the top
of his voice,* What have you to do with me, Jesus, Son of
the Most High God? *. . .*

For he [Christ] had said to him, Come out of the man,
you unclean spirit! *. . .*

*Now there on the hillside a great herd of swine was
feeding. Mark 5:2, 6-8, 11*

Unclean spirits,
who possess
some Israelites,
bow down
before Jesus.
Caligulas
from the lowest
pit of hell,
believe in Jesus
proclaim him
the Son
of the Most
High God,
ask a favor,
obey.

Jesus
chooses apostles
who believe
somewhat,
observe in awe
as he heals the blind,
hear him call Lazarus
from the grave,
observe the soldiers
come with clubs,
see the Judas kiss.
They see Jesus
heal an ear,
run.

BUT JESUS CAUGHT TWO FISH

He [Jesus] saw James son of Zebedee and his brother John,
who were in their boat mending the nets. Mark 1:19

You do not mess with fishermen
after a long night of fishing
with empty boats,
mending their nets, counting

their loss. If you poke an angry fire,
stand back for it will flare out
like fire arrow. If you are strolling
along the shore of the ocean

and come upon such fishermen,
no small talk, no pleasantries.
Just hurry past as though late
for synagogue. But Jesus stops,

You have no fish, I see. Come,
follow me. I can't believe
he doesn't know better. But James
and John, the Sons of Thunder,

undisturbed, leave father Zebedee, boat,
nets, and follow the provincial dolt.
Their father stands alone—sonless.

CANA AND FIVE JARS OF WATER

They have no wine. . . . Now standing there were six stone water jars . . . each holding twenty or thirty gallons. John 2:3, 6

Rabbi and the twelve,
like those come
off a fast, drink

from vats with
open spigot,
wise to free

wedding wine,
not sipping *lentissimo*
but like fishermen *capriccio*,

while disaster looms
as the gaggle of guests
snack

on fried apricots dipped
in honey. Men
dance with the groom,

the women with the bride.
Even beggars dance
'til reluctant dawn.

But Mother Mary hears
disturbing rumors
of wine failure

and tells her unready son,
who balks. *Woman,
the hour the Father*

*decreed has not
yet come. But
at your word,*

*I carry out
plans
from forever—*

*now slightly
bent. I'll annoy
pale water
to flagrant red.*

DON'T PUT ETERNITY ON HOLD

To another he [Jesus] said, Follow me. *But he said,*
Lord, first let me go and bury my father. *But Jesus
said to him,* Let the dead bury their own dead; but
as for you, go and proclaim the kingdom of God.
Luke 9:59, 60

I'm speechless. Though
the man's unknown to me,
I hear, *Follow me!*
A command to leave all

before my father dies
and I can bury him.
That's impiety!
If I say *"later,"*

that unreasonable man will say,
unfit. But if I say, *"yes,"*
everything's at risk.
All other loyalties must yield,

it seems. Perhaps he's saying,
one does not put eternal life
on hold. He invites me
to lose my life, promises pain,

invites me to love father
and mother less. He calls me
to preach distressing words
to the bored, to torch

with new-fallen fire
the antiseptic righteous,
the yawning sated.

I start now . . .
or not at all.

THE BATS

We're chosen,
God-anointed,
who know where the cook
keeps the bread and how

to slice it. We're bats
with expensive but compromised
radar systems,
called to judge others

whose shameless secrets
we know. Like others
we slouch, stumble
on our shoe-strings

while trying to steady
those who stand upright.
We're a torch lighting up
back alleys, bars on the wharf.

We hold the keys
to unlock—or lock—
the stabbings in Dinky Town,
the insider trading on Wall Street.

But bats in our own cave,
we hang upside down
with the other bats
and smell our droppings.

A BANQUET FOR SCOUNDRELS

He was eating with sinners and tax collectors. Mark 2:16

Jesus gives a banquet. To my right embezzlers,
robbers, oppressors of widows, priests
who visit whores at night; to my left, pimps,
ax murderers, money-lenders, liars, cheats,

all come to Capernaum for a feast.
He moves from guest to guest;
a word here, a smile there.
These are his kind of people.

JUST A CRUMB FROM YOUR TABLE

Unless you see signs and wonders you will not believe.
John 4:48

Everyone in Cana talks about how
you changed six large urns of water
into finest wine. Dare
an uncircumcised Gentile ask

a favor? I do not play the heavy
as though you'd be impressed
that a centurion commands
a hundred Roman soldiers.

You could ask, *Since when*
does an officer of an occupying force
ask favors? True, I wear
no prayer shawl, have never laid

a spotless lamb upon the Jewish altar.
But I was told Leviticus decrees,
You shall love the alien
as yourself. My little son is dying

twenty miles away in Capernaum.
You could ride down
on a military horse,
lay your hands on Publius

and be back in Cana
before your disciples
sip tomorrow's evening wine
and pray the Shema.

You scold me like an acned teenager
who pants for extravaganzas.
I ask for a crumb.
My little boy is dying.

YOUR CHOICE

*Someone gave a great dinner and invited many. At the time for
the dinner he sent his slave to say to those who had been invited,*
Come; for everything is ready now. *But they all alike began to
make excuses. Luke 14:16-18.*

Now they make excuses. Not flimsy ones
but events they could've foreseen.
You do not marry Tuesday and know nothing
of it Monday. I've invited you many times

and always excuses. It's insulting!
Now shanks of lamb lie on the platter,
wine poured in my best goblets and I am shamed
with an empty banquet hall. For months

I've planned this feast: pigeon eggs,
grouse livers, roasted locusts with vinegar,
walnut bread still warm. Now hear this!
Not one drop of my Hebron wine will ever

flow down your throats. I'm not a weak flame.
If you blow out my candle, you'll sit in the dark.
By choice you exclude yourselves. And yes,
it matters whether you come or not. But be under

no illusion; it will not all turn out as you
   wish. . . .
Life's not a game of chess where,
after I check your King, we box the pieces
to start again tomorrow. No second game.

YOU ALWAYS GAVE ME LEFTOVERS

[The elder son] answered his father, Listen! For all these years I
have been working like a slave for you . . . you have never given
me even a young goat so that I might celebrate with my friends.
But when this son of yours comes back . . . you killed the fatted
calf for him. *Luke 15:29-30*

> You seem surprised your favorite son came home.
> The temple stones will die before he stays away.
> Gold gone, he cannot buy the booze or rent a gal.
>
> He's home to gull you once again.
> Your horny stud has cast his seed as though
> the granary's bottomless and he'll live forever.
>
> He plucked you clean and now he's back to glean.
> You love your horny bull more than me,
>   though he's
> a mask behind a mask and you are blind.
>
> I'm up at dawn. I shear your flock of sheep.
> I keep your mules, I feed your ox. Your rules
> on how you want your beasts and barns and fields
>
> attended I have scrupulously kept.
> You spoil a slave if you give him money.
> Do I expect too much? If once, just once,

you gave me a goat to celebrate a festive night
and dance with friends around the fire with
harp and tambourines! Father, you begot two sons,

remember? So why did you drain my sap to fill his
    pail?
Father, go. Dance until your bunions shriek.
If the sheep-skin still has wine, please fill

your cup. Then stop the music, stop the dance.
And put your arm around your favorite's neck.
Raise high your cup to toast your only son.

PART III

CAN LOVE BE UNCONDITIONAL?

Now his elder son . . . refused to go [into the banquet]. . . .
[Their father said,] We had to celebrate and rejoice, because this
brother of yours was dead and has come to life; he was lost and
has been found. *Luke 15:25, 28, 32*

> Your brother is not a piece of garbage, mutton
>   bone
> or apple core, that I should toss him in the garbage
>   pit.
> You refuse to share a banquet for a brother come
>   home.
> You can't stand outside while we celebrate inside!
>
> You both clobbered me. Your brother asked his
>   portion
> while I live, as though I failed at dying. And you!
> Did I breed a mercenary son who guards
> his share of drachmas before he digs my grave?
>
> When you beget sons they'll make within the
>   narrows
> of your heart great seas of love flowing on below
> with quiet constancy, while your anger storms
> above. I loved the boy before he asked, I loved him
>
> while he asked, I loved him lost, I love him found.
> A father cannot qualify his love by *if* or *when*.

The two of you belong to who I am, as life exists
as one in vine and branch. You're a blistered
    branch

that I can cure by touch. If your brother axed his
    limb
from our vine, I'll graft it on again. But, son,
I'm not a banker who gives out only gold deposited,
not a paymaster pinching with cranky care each
    coin

he owes lest he overpay: gardener, twenty drachmas;
carpenter, eighteen denarii; shepherd, ten shekels.
You ask too little, son. You cannot weigh love by
    scale
as a butcher weighs a shank of lamb.

ONLY COLD WATER
AND A BEEF SANDWICH

Love your enemies and pray for those who persecute you.
Matthew 5:44

That bastard! That creepy son-of-a-bitch
mechanic who pats my carburetor,
$800 a pat.

The sign outside reads
SAM'S NEIGHBORHOOD GARAGE
So he's the neighbor I'm supposed to love,
turn the other cheek!
Fat chance!

Then there's that slimy lawyer
who feints and dodges
and snows me with legalese
greased with a threat.
Him too?

Lord, if loving cheats is the new Torah
by which you'll measure me,
I'm lost.

I'll give a cup of cold water
to that thirsty mechanic
if he were dying in the desert
and a beef sandwich
to that hungry lawyer,
if he were stranded on an island.

But love
without the boundary stone
of an *if?*

MY FATHER

A needy, hollow-eyed, sharp-looking wretch, a living-dead man.
Shakespeare, The Comedy of Errors

The snow was new upon the northern ground
that March, a foot of tumbled crisp geometries,
white patience laid soft across Dad's new Ford,
the company car now parked upon the street.

Who at fourteen has not jingled
car keys in a pocket of dirty jeans,
the golden spurs of the unneeded shave,
that first defiant beer in the pubescent night?

The key rages the motor into life,
the car lurches through the swirl,
I, a Dakota samurai on a steed of steel,
a city cowboy for fifty feet of freedom,

shirring off Dad's fender on Ruben Krebsbach's
car parked just ahead. I was suckled
by wolves, ran with the pack, but now
my feral glands stutter with fear.

How does one tell the father of eight wild ones,
each a jingler of the mystic keys,
hot for the road and great gulps of the world,
how tell him of his fenderless car and live?

He put his arm around my neck and said,
Son, it was your turn to wreck the car.

DON'T MEASURE LOVE
AS YOU WOULD ARSENIC

But we had to celebrate and rejoice, because this brother of
yours was dead and has come to life; he was lost and has
been found. Luke 15:32

Son, you are always with me.
All my pastures, granges, granaries
all are yours, have ever been.
You are my very self.
But for the living owner

I did not blow the shofar.
You are right, of course:
My love is tacky, untidy.
But you mistake to balance love,
to measure it by level teaspoons,

like a chemist weighing arsenic,
no excess.

When the grave throws up a son
I have a commotion of love,
a proper father malady,

a three-alarm riot
in the heart.
I dance,
I sing,
I lift my cup.

AGGRESSIVE MERCY

But while he [younger son] was still far off, his father saw him and was filled with compassion; he ran and put his arms around him and kissed him. Luke 15:20

You have to say this
for the old man—
he let me make the wrong decision.

He pleaded but no coercion.
Without pinching each coin
he counted out the drachmas.

May's red poppies led me
to June's Eros avenue:
painted women, boozy nights,

and soon an empty purse.
No real meal
for days.

I stand in pig's swill
Up to my ankles
and ache

to eat the slop.
The corn cob between my toes.
Remember the goat meat,

the melons and date breads
on Father's table.
What the swaggering wisdom

of testosterone loses,
an empty stomach wins.
I'll go back and piece together

the tomorrows I've destroyed.
I rehearse repentance rhetoric
as I go. If I find the right words

he might forgive.

At the bend of the road
I see my father running,
toward me, weeping. We embrace
and fall laughing to our knees,
his tears drown my little speech.

The tomorrows are already mine.

PURGING THE TEMPLE

He entered the temple and began to drive out those who
were selling and those who were buying in the temple.
Mark 11:15

We scribes and Pharisees
know he's been a troublemaker
up north in Galilee:
badmouths temple sacrifice,
eats with street walkers,
smelly beggars,
and tax-pirates who prey
on widows.

He comes into the temple
with twelve assorted losers.
This new Goliath makes a whip
from rope used to bind a pigeon cage
and like some mad Ezekiel
trashes buyers and sellers
who rape the house of God.
He topples cages, releases birds,
whacks beasts,
upturns tables of silver denarii.
Can't we offer sacrifice to our God
without the tinkle of coins?

Pilgrims panic
toward the gate, some slip and fall
on brown pellets dropped
by sheep and goats.

He's dead meat.

JESUS AND THE PAPARAZZI

He [Jesus] said to them [apostles], Come away to a deserted place all by yourselves and rest a while. . . . *Now many saw them going and recognized them, and they hurried there on foot from all the towns and arrived ahead of them. Mark 6:31, 33*

Exhausted from many preacher words,
Jesus boards a boat
to take his apostles,
eagles who've lost their tail feathers,
to a deserted place to rest,

but villages and hamlets along the shore
empty out: bakers who left their bread to rise,
housewives with snotty babies
on the hip, prostitutes ready for the long night,

more than 5,000 racing along the shore
so as not to lose his boat
in Galilean mists.
When we land jostling, clawing hordes

that cling like relentless vines;
all want front seats to see
the prophetic extravaganza.
But Jesus sits and teaches kingdom truths:

pluck out eyes, cut off hands,
love your enemy, forgive the unforgivable.
Late afternoon,
we suggest he send the crowd away

to buy their bread from peasants.
He teases, *Give them food yourselves.*
We tease back, *You advised,*
take no money in your belts.

He blesses five loaves and two fish
we find among the crowd.
More than 5,000 eat their fill
with twelve baskets left over.

If you pray for bread with empty hand,
why are you surprised
that God who made the sun and stars
places ten loaves in your apron?

MARK, YOU HAVE TO DO BETTER

They saw a young man . . . sitting on the right side.
Mark 16:5

For sixteen chapters
I see him walk the waters
of fury, hear, *Take up*
your bed and walk,
watch the woman sneak
behind his back to reach
a cheeky hand to steal
the healing of us all.
I smell the kitchen smell
of bread become his body.

Mark, you are a full-stomached
tabby with a mouse,
playing us for sport.

You promised, I was willing
to be caught, but in chapter
sixteen you fogged the ending.

On the first day of the week,
when Easter sun was new,
the women saw the stone
was rolled away, a single
angel sitting with his skinny

message, like the personals
in the Boston Globe.
He's risen. Tell Peter,
Go to Galilee.
You will see him.

That's it?
No John and Peter racing
toward the tomb, no Magdalene
to grab his risen feet,
no fish fry by the lake.

At one time five hundred saw him.
Ten times the Risen Christ appeared
and all you can manage is
one measly angel.

SPECIAL PLACES FOR SPECIAL BOYS

*The mother of the sons of Zebedee came to him with
her sons, and kneeling before him, she asked a favor of
him. . . . Declare that these two sons of mine will sit, one
at your right hand, and one at your left, in your kingdom.*
Matthew 20:20, 21

This stage-door mother
omits none of the ritual
—bows, smiles, prostrations—
as she elbows through, reaching
behind her skirts to pull
the Sons of Thunder forward,
(as if small boys)
to the traveling tragedian going
to Jerusalem one last time.

She gathers shawl,
tucks a wisp of hair,
speaks her high ambition,
Rabbi, let my two sons sit
on gilded thrones
on your right and left
in your kingdom.

*Mother, the thrones are not mine
to give.
But be assured,
your boys will drink my cup
of blood, be baptized deep
in the desolation of my pain.*

Thanks, Ma.

SHALL I DANCE FOR YOU?

*When his daughter Herodias came in and danced, she
pleased Herod and his guests. Mark 6:21*

An unhooded falcon with unsheathed
claws thrown high in the air,
I soar, swoop, stamp,

flounce my skirts, twirl,
flutter my veil, pound
the tambourine, wink,

ruffle my fluffy hair,
shake a smiling "No"
at paunchy Bika bar Ben

(three hairs across the dome
like three nomads lost
in the desert), slowly pouring

the reddest wine on the red
floor, a wave offering
to my divinity. I glide

between rows of couches,
bow low before a tipsy
Herod. His payment

will be dear. No promise
of a new veil,
no sack
of greasy shekels, no half a kingdom.

I want blood.

STONES ARE CHEAP

The scribes and Pharisees brought a woman who had been caught in adultery. John 8:3

Suddenly the door flew open and I was caught
in mid-ecstasy. Shame, terror,
I'm pushed down Jaffa Street half-naked

to the middle of the throng gathered round
the prophet teaching outside the Temple.
I stand before the prophet while scribes

and Pharisees cite Moses' stoning law:
Sin certain, text clear, Torah-stones lie ready.
What say you? In front of Pharisees

Jesus bends down to doodle in the dust
with one contemptuous finger. While
Torah-guardians insist I die

he grabs a stone, and walking
in front of my accusers, offers it to each,
Let the man guilty of no sexual sin throw

the first stone. Older men leave first,
then the younger, until Misery and Mercy
alone remain. The prophet asks,

Where are your accusers?

JUDGMENT

He [Moses] looked, and the bush was blazing, yet it was
not consumed. Then Moses said, I must turn aside and look
at this great sight, and see why the bush is not burned up.
Exodus 3:23

Rather judge me by the law of Sinai
engraved by the finger of God
on tablets of stone
than by the holiness standing behind it.

I do not speak of antiseptic rectitude
but the glory which burns
like a bush not consumed,
the absolute autonomy of fire,

which appears as a marvel to one
who sees and approaches.
Then the Fire scolds, *Do not come near.*

No, let it be the cold stone of the Law.

THE PROBLEM OF PAIN

*A great windstorm arose . . . but he [Jesus] was in the
stern, asleep on the cushion. Mark 4:37-38*

The text must be corrupt.
A fourth-century scribe
dropped off to sleep
and smudged the ink

just after he wrote of thunder,
waves breaking over the side
almost swamping the boat,

the Master there
on the stern, on the high
after-deck, asleep
on a pillow,
of goose down
and feathers?

*The foxes have lairs,
birds of the air their nests,
but the Son of Man has
nowhere to lay his head.*

But now the text says,
during a gale—
the boat aswamp
with fury,

his friends almost
lost in the savage sea.
Now, he finds his comfort
slumbering on a pillow.

Does God sleep
on goose down?
While we perish,
God dozes?

NO WORMY LAZARUS

Six days before the Passover Jesus came to Bethany. . . .
When the great crowd of the Jews learned that he was there,
they came not only because of Jesus but also to see Lazarus.
John 12:1, 9

When I waddle from the tomb,
I'm astonished as Peter unwinds
the mummy linen strips.

On the veranda
my sisters throw
a banquet and they

wonder about the difference
between living
in God's glory

and walking
in God's shadow.
Friends say a talking

mummy need not argue.
Do I have grave truths to tell?
High priests walk in

and stand behind our couches,
asking themselves,
what can logic do with resurrection?

These priests protect the sacred scrolls
and see in my rising
scattered temple stones and Torah ashes.

No more sprinkled blood
of bulls upon the altar.
I hear these priests

talking treachery into the wind
as they leave to walk toward Jerusalem.
The one who called Lazarus

from the tomb must die.
For a man who would destroy the temple
no more quibbles about legality.

And then we'll deal with Lazarus.
After we dispatch him,
we'll burn the corpse.

LAZARUS EMBARRASSED

The chief priests planned to put Lazarus to death as well, since it was on account of him that many of the Jews were deserting and were believing in Jesus. John 12:10-11

Really now, it's so embarrassing!
Clumsy, to say the least.
You thought the Lord did it for me,

while, in fact, it was for you.
A sacrament snatched cold
from four days dead

in hillside tomb,
returned from the back of beyond
to insist again upon Jesus' obvious gift:

I am his sign, his pledge and prophecy,
his down payment on what is yet
to come, and you would send me

back again, this time to some
opaque non-existence.
You have seen death slam the door

decisively against all retreat, but also
that carpenter from nowhere
turn back, undo, cancel my decay.

For you he undid the terror
of my death, unslammed the door,
unrung the tolling bell, and yet,

dyspeptic dolts, you hesitate?
What other parting of the sea
do you demand before you say your "yes"?

QUESTIONS FOR LAZARUS

*[A great crowd of Jews] came not only because of Jesus but
also to see Lazarus. John 12:9*

I've no tomb dust
upon my sleeves,
no victory crown of celery leaves
upon my head,

no lingering whiff of my decay
when I sit down at table
with droves watching,
watching through the windows

at the newly dead back
from Abraham's bosom.
The Eleven have questions
Jesus left unanswered.

What had I seen beyond the flesh?
The glory of God as on Mount Sinai?
Angels who guard the shadow of God?
Are the saints ever sated?

Were you sent back to say
death is dead?

Will you die again?

THE DEATH OF JOSEPH

Precious in the sight of the LORD is the death of his
faithful ones. Psalm 116:15

I'm in the kitchen
washing the evening dishes
when I hear a clatter
in the shop.
Nothing unusual;
Joseph drops clamps
or boards occasionally.
But when it's too quiet
I poke my head inside.
There he is on his back
on the sawdust,
hands clutching his chest,
still breathing. I scream
for help but Jesus is out dancing
with friends. I run next door
for Rachel and Jacob, send
for my son. We get Joseph
to his bed. No doctor
in the village so I send
for midwife Sarah
who loosens his shirt,
cools his brow with a wet rag.

Jesus rushes into the room.
We stand beside the bed, praying
Psalm twenty-one:
You set a crown
of fine gold on his head.
You gave length of days
forever and ever.
Joseph opens his eyes,
tries to speak
but there is no sound.
He drops his right hand
at his side.

PART IV

DISCARDED

My God, my God, why have you forsaken me?
Matthew 27:46

At Thursday supper
all apostles vowed fidelity
as we passed around

the covenant cup—before
my first betrayer left.
Two hours later

in the Garden of Olives,
all fled, gone
as quickly as sound

from a shofar's horn.
For three years
I dropped miracles

like sand falling through
fingers of my hand:
turned water

into expensive wine,
gave sight to a man born
blind, stilled the stormy sea.

Memories decay like waves.
While I sweat blood
I asked to be spared,

but you answered
with sour silence there
beneath the barren olive trees.

JUDAS IN LOVE

Then Judas Iscariot . . . went to the chief priests in order to betray him to them. Mark 14:10

After I receive the bread
his body, the wine his blood,
I leave, and he does not expose me.
When I close the door

behind me the light
of the upper room is blotted out,
hinges squeak as wood
against wood makes a thud

of finality. It is finished.
I weep as I walk
toward the temple gate. Still,
it must be done:

Beat plowshares into swords
to drive the Romans out.

Betrayal of the man I love
pours drops of dread into my wine.
But if you drink wine, you press grapes.
The Romans must go.

SO IT HAS COME TO THIS?

O Lord, you have enticed me, and I was enticed; you have overpowered me, and you have prevailed. Jeremiah 20:7

Did I hear correctly?
You bore me up on eagles' wings,
and now it has come to truth?

If you stoop to searching hearts,
who will defend me from my lies?
Do you really want my blood?

Your truth is the trap door
my dreary truth falls through—
but my rope is not long enough.

No one is innocent,
no one righteous, no not one.
All have turned aside.

All our lives need the secret
Nicodemus night, the side door in,
the cloaked confessional.

Even truth in God stumbles,
cannot attain untainted purity.
Seduced by mercy, ravished
at the door by compassion.

JUDAS' PECK UPON THE CHEEK

Now Judas, who betrayed him, also knew the place [Garden of Gethsemane], because Jesus often met there with his disciples.
John 18:2

No need to grope along the garden wall
as I've seen blind men do. I've been here
before but now I come with a fresh hole
in my heart, a wounded love in my breast

and a fresh kiss upon my lips.
When I just now betrayed the man I love,
I strangled the heart of who I am.
Still, one cannot deny necessity.

I must cut the bonds, become un-chosen
so we can expel the thugs
who defile our sacred land. The Romans
stand tall, like pyramids in Egypt,

they foul our temple with military banners,
gouge pockets full of taxes, taken from those
who sip nettle gruel and eat crusts
of moldy bread. For thirty silver coins

the holy priests bought my tender peck
upon the cheek. In the light of the guards'
torches I kissed my Jesus beneath the olive trees.

—The bitterest gall of all, he loves me still.

JUDAS' WIFE

*Do we not have the right to be accompanied
by a believing wife, as do the other apostles
and the brothers of the Lord and Cephas?*
1 Corinthians 9:5

On black nights my Judas meets
in back rooms with other zealots
who want the Romans out.
Talk, talk, talk, but nothing happens.

These Davids have only
fistfuls of smoke to sling
at their Goliaths. Besides,
the God of Israel sleeps.

Then the Rabbi Jesus chose my man
to stride beside him. Judas,
whom I love, has tangles of tics,
mists within, walks along edges, shifts
like slag. He has a hard time
being a person. Certainly
not chosen for his piety, though
like the others, he wears
his prayer shawl over his bald spot.

The Rabbi heals withered hands,
exorcises demons,
raises Lazarus (my man stood
on his left); miracles drop
like broadcast barley.

At Passover Judas stops talking
because he grasps this liberation
will have no siege machines,
no javelins. And the Romans stay.

The one who looks
beyond tomorrow
for some diaphanous kingdom,
demanding we love
our enemies,
must be pushed aside.

Judas wants a kingdom today,
the promised hundredfold cold
upon the palms of his hands.

But Judas takes the thirty pieces
of silver. Not too much,
considering what they bought.

Suddenly the whole affair gets
out of hand, and we're on Calvary.

PILATE'S WIFE

Have nothing to do with that innocent man, for today I
have suffered a great deal because of a dream about him.
Matthew 27:19

You contend that I chatter away,
but say nothing; besides you do
not believe in dreams. Also you have

no time to listen. But once, just once,
hear me. I talk a lot, but you know
I never interfere. Right?

You made the gates to the court
high enough for mounted camels.
Last night this man came

to the palace. As he was about
to pass through the gate, it began
to grow higher, higher,

making space for some
cosmic loneliness, some
bottomless light beyond

knowing or negation. He faded out
and faded in, but had the sharp
edge of reality. He looked at me,

asked nothing, and was gone.
Then, clearer still, I saw a lamb
standing slain on a hill

of triumphant blood.
I have known terror
and I have known joy

but never both at once.
Pilate dear, truth stands
before you waiting to be judged.
Don't wash your hands.

TO TOUCH THE SILENCE OF GOD

There are none nearer to God in this life than those haters and blasphemers of him, nor any sons more pleasing and beloved by him. Martin Luther

No doubt Luther had Jesus' blasphemy in mind, the cry of dereliction from the cross. Gerhard Forde

Why? I cry my blasphemy
from an emptiness
so heavy it weighs more

than that boulder in front of me.
In terror of the heavy cost
I sweat blood,

I asked you
to spare me,
still you brought me

to this void.
You broke
the bruised reed,

quenched the flickering flame
of the wick burnt
to a stub.

You called me,
walked away
ignored my pleas

and left me alone
nails in my hands.
You left me alone.

IT IS FINISHED

Then Jesus cried again with a loud voice and he breathed his last.
Matthew 27:50

I invoke Einstein. On the cross,
time is slowed, space stretched.

One needs to be both in time and eternity,
to grasp the enormity of what happens.

Without stretched-out space how could infinity
have been emptied? How could a pendulum be
    slowed

enough so that the narrowing walls of faltering
    time
leaves enough of a hole of measuredness to let

the cross beams through; otherwise, how could
    you
in time bleed dry one already empty?

How could you in space
degrade one already stripped?

How could one grasp the dread mystery
which, like the universe, has no edge?

WHO ARE YOU, LORD?

When you have lifted up the Son of Man, then you will realize that I am he. John 8:28

How, Lord, do you explain
yourself? In fact, you never

try except to give enigmas.
You hand the visually impaired

opaque glasses,
through which only

peripheral vision
sees mists.

You give a cane
for the cripple

to poke the path
up some luminous Tabor

to hear secret words
too high,

too implacably one
for us who know

by dividing. You only say
that when Wisdom is lifted up

a fool and bleeds,
we'll understand.

THE DEATH OF A MONK

Brother Dietrich Reinhart, OSB:
May 17, 1949–December 29, 2008

He died the slow melanoma death.
Then the cancer suddenly ran wild
like fierce anger consuming
its own destruction.—He urged us

to run beyond our bones,
keep the great books open,
remember to serve is to rule,
no crust of bread will be in vain.

Falling snow lays a blanket
of cold bewilderment
as the dark-stained casket arrives.
Father John hammered it together

from pines along the ridge. Monks,
remembering that death crouches
at the door to Light, gather
in the baptistery around the simple box

with an ordinary pillow. We listen
to Brother James read the Rule
which calls monks to listen
for silences, to kneel with our hearts,

teaches where to dig for treasure.
The gaunt finger of John the Baptist,
bronze burnished gold by years
of touching, points nowhere.

But Dietrich knows the Way.

PETER THE MORNING AFTER

*Our chief priests and leaders handed him over to be
condemned to death and crucified him. But we had hoped
that he was the one to redeem Israel. Luke 24:20-21*

I, Peter, the solid rock, wobble,
though chosen to confirm the others

should they falter. Today rivers run backwards,
mountains collapse into hollows.

Hammered nails pierce our universe
and all Jesus' miracles leak out.

Did the hungry eat fresh foam and were twelve
    baskets
of bread left over, vapor? When we rolled the
    stone

across the entrance to his tomb
did we bury the New Jerusalem,

and its roads paved with pure gold,
transparent as mountain brook?

Will we ever have God's name written
on our foreheads?

Jesus left questions. Is the emptying of blood the
answer?
I'm going fishing.

ONLY WHAT I CAN TOUCH

Unless I [Thomas] see the mark of the nails in his hands, and put
my finger in the mark of the nails and my hand in his side, I will
not believe. John 20:25

Like the trash crucified on either side, Jesus went
in nakedness, blood, and a loud cry.
And I myself rolled the stone to the entrance of
   his tomb.

Two days later, I was at home with wife
and seven children eating dried mutton strips
spread with ghee, when, the others claimed
—claimed—the dead Lord came
and showed the nail holes in his hands and feet
and the deep gash in his side.

I'm supposed to believe that?
I demand proof: no ersatz body,
no metaphysical spook to replace the solid hand
which broke the crust of bread and placed it
on my palm. I demand skin.

A week passes, and I am with them, doors bolted,
windows secured as though Pilate's guards
searched for us. Without a knock upon the door
or tap upon the window the Crucified stands
before us and offers to my unbelieving fingers
the nail holes in his hands
the gash between his ribs.

I fall upon my knees.

TABORS AND CANAS

Why are you cast down, O my soul, and why are you disquieted within me? Hope in God; for I shall again praise him, my help and my God. Psalm 42:11

Of course, Lord, you've heard it all before,
the printed praises in the choir book
flung out across monastic chancels,
the dull muster of tired pieties,
two thousand years of warmed-over song,
the high melismatic rhetoric of Lauds,
rousing snow and sleet, sparrow and eagle
to shout our inattentive adoration,
the same yesterday, today, and tomorrow.

All our Tabors seem pits,
all our Canas snacks,
as we crank out the predictable,
pre-cooked, pre-packaged Glory to God.

But you know our hearts from afar,
you know we stutter
and we stumble.

We would not exchange one day in your courts
for a thousand in the palaces of princes.

IN PRAISE OF HESITATIONS

Unless I . . . put my finger in the mark of the nails and my hand in his side, I will not believe. John 20:25

Qualms never more eloquent
than that first day when
absent Thomas who hadn't seen the Lord yet,
proposed scientific controls

like touch and feel, put his finger
into the wound, to reach
beyond the body's bloody gash
to the scandal of a "yes."

Not a storm God, the Master
rips no "yes" by the root
with the lightning of his arm.
But to hesitate is not to Judas.

TWO FOOLS ON THE WAY TO EMMAUS

Are you the only stranger in Jerusalem who does not know the things that have taken place there in these days? Luke 24:18.

Gravel noise. A stranger sidled up as Jacob and
   I walked
and talked. He came from Jerusalem but knew
   nothing
of Jesus and betrayal, nothing of nails and
   nakedness

and the scream at the end. We spoke of some,
   smelling
of temple rectitude, who tore his flesh to the
   bone.
Instead of defeating pagans, they nailed this
   Prophet

to a cross between two thieves and turned our
   hope
to despair. Nor had the stranger heard of silly
   women,
demented with grief, who said he lives.

They had touched his feet and he had protested.
What everybody in Jerusalem knew the stranger
   did not.
Fools, he turned on us as if we were naughty
   children

caught playing war in the Holy of Holies,
　　You know nothing.
Through his words the stranger marched us out
　　of Egypt,
talked us through walls of Red Sea water,
　　by Sinai's mount

of fire into Bethlehem, Cana and Capernaum
　　and up that awful hill.
Not in perfumed purple silks upon a gilded
　　chariot
comes God's Chosen Servant but in blood and
　　nakedness.

The stranger's words were long tongs that stirred
our burned-out cinders into flame. Jacob and
　　I lived
alive inside the story. In Emmaus he walked

as if his destination were farther on but we
　　begged
he sup with us. The moment he broke and blessed
　　the bread we knew.
And he vanished.

STUMBLING TOWARD DAMASCUS

I myself will show him [Paul] how much he must suffer.
Acts 9:16

So untypical of God to be abrupt.
Jesus extinguished the pillar of fire,
then lit the way into thick darkness
where God dwells. Without warning

snatched, phylacteries snipped off,
stripped, the Temple ripped from me.
The Torah scroll erased,
seven Menorah candles extinguished.

I shed the Law
as a snake sheds its skin.
Before I hit the ground,
my enemies made friends.
my life subverted,

scattered like broadcast lentil seeds,
I'm the sanctuary guard on duty
before the temple gate captured
by one who has no sword.

My boast transubstantiated
into shame, blasphemy into adoration.
Now I sit among the toddlers
to learn my newest alphabet,

drudge to spell new words.
The Lamb stands slain.

And in its face I see the mirror
of my death and its doxology.

TELL US ABOUT
THE ABSOLUTE START

In the beginning was the Word. John 1:1

When I was old the children sat
me down and gathered round
to ask about absolute beginnings,
as though I, John, predated
time, born before rocks
were hard, fire burned.

Tell us how it was
before chaos and void
covered the deep,
before the wind from God swept
over the face of the waters,
before Yahweh walked through the garden
in the cool of the evening breeze,
How was it
when only "I AM" was there
and no one to listen.

I have no unveiled knowledge;
but when we peasants gathered
around the campfire
we used to sing an epic
of how God tarried long
in the doorway
before saying the secret Word
that was with God forever,

using the spoken but unspent
speech, icon of splendor,
as the pattern for the primal parents
and everything come into being.

The Word spoken but unspent,
hammered his tent pegs deep
into the loam on our side.
He walked among us
dropping wonders as mist.
Our eyes have seen the glory pass
the boundaries of Bethlehem
as we reach across to taste the truth.

What was said became flesh
and bone.

UNWRAPPING THE GIFT

Whoever believes in the Son has eternal life. John 3:36

Like a Christmas present,
eternal life, received, unopened, but mine.
When death pulls the silver ribbons,

tears aside the red-green paper I'll see
for the first time the gift
for years already mine: the Galilees of
    consequence,

the untangled splendor. Before I believed
but never suspected.
The deceits of the Lord are deep.

NOTES ON THE POEMS

"Unequal Equals"

Though the meaning of this archaic rite is disputed, I take the view that this covenant ceremony depicts the blood bond between the Lord and Abram and a consequent dismemberment if one of the parties is unfaithful to the covenant.

"Your Choice"

Luke 14:16-18 is paralleled by Matthew 22:1-22. Besides the many comforting teachings in this gospel, Jesus also makes difficult demands on his disciples, among which are aspects of the wedding banquet parable.

Harvard exegete N. T. Wright, commenting on the text from Matthew, writes, "We want to hear a nice story about God throwing the party open to everyone. We want . . . to be 'inclusive,' to let everyone in. We don't want to know about judgment on the wicked, or about demanding standards of holiness. . . . God wants us to be grown up, not babies, and part of being grown up is that we learn that actions have consequences, that moral choices matter. . . . The great, deep mystery of God's forgiveness isn't the same as saying that whatever we do isn't really important because it'll all work out somehow" (*Matthew for Everyone,* part 2 [Louisville, KY: Westminster-John Knox, 2004], 82, 83).

"Can Love Be Unconditional?"

The first two lines of the sixth stanza refer to the Parable of the Vine and the Branches. Jesus says, "I am the vine and you are the branches" (John 15:5). The fruit of belief in Jesus is eternal life, which is the life of Jesus.

As Sandra Schneiders writes, "This divine life, already enjoyed in this world, makes [persons] children of God (see John 1:12,13), brothers and sisters of Jesus (see John 20:17), who can call Jesus' God and Father their own God and Father. It makes them participants, even now, in the life shared by Jesus and God in the Holy Spirit. It makes them living branches of Jesus, the true vine" (*Written That You May Believe* [New York: Herder & Herder, 1999], 14).

"Mark, You Have to Do Better"

A number of scholars have expressed surprise that Mark would have ended his gospel so abruptly at 16:8. It is possible, if unlikely, that Mark intended to end the gospel at 16:8. The early church must have thought it unlikely too as three attempts were made to give a fuller ending from other sources. The author of these three expansions, one Shorter, the other Longer, and the Freer Logion, was not Mark himself but some other person. Though not of Markan origin, the church has received the Shorter and Longer Endings as authentically inspired and canonical. Perhaps the Longer Ending might have been written in the second century and added, thinking it might be a better ending. For further information on the text of the three endings, see John R. Donahue and Daniel J. Harrington, *The Gospel of Mark* (Collegeville, MN: Liturgical Press, 2002), 462–64.

"Stones Are Cheap"

"Although Jesus' challenge is not explicitly stated, it is most likely that it refers to sin in the sexual area" (Francis Maloney, *The Gospel of John* [Collegeville, MN: Liturgical Press, 1998], 261).

For my line "until Misery and Mercy / alone remain," I'm indebted to St. Augustine: "Only two remain, the wretched woman (*misera*) and the incarnation of mercy (*misericordia*)" (*Commentary on the Gospel of John*, 33.5).